Sports Shots Collector's Book 6

DON MATTINGLY

by Devra Newberger

SCHOLASTIC INC.

New York • Toronto • London • Auckland • Sydney

For Richard and Jeremy

Photo Credits
Cover photo: © Duomo/Adam J. Stoltman. Inside front cover: (top) © Duomo/Bryan Yablonsky 1989; (bottom) © Duomo/Steven E. Sutton 1988. Page iv: © Duomo/Bryan Yablonsky 1988. Page 4: Bruce L. Schwartzman. Page 8: Bruce L. Schwartzman. Page 14: Bruce L. Schwartzman. Page 17: © Duomo/Al Tielemans 1988. Page 20: © Duomo/ Al Tielemans 1988. Page 24: © Duomo/Bryan Yablonsky 1989. Page 28: © Duomo/Adam J. Stoltman 1984. Page 33: ACCM Communication Industries, Inc. Page 38: © Duomo/Bryan Yablonsky 1988. Inside back cover: (top) Bruce L. Schwartzman; (bottom) © Duomo 1984.

Design by Design Five, New York.

ISBN 0-590-45197-9
Copyright © 1991 by Scholastic Inc.
All rights reserved. Published by Scholastic Inc.,
730 Broadway, New York, NY 10003

12 11 10 9 8 7 6 5 4 3 2   1 2 3 4 5 6/9
Printed in the U.S.A.   10
First Scholastic printing, September 1991

CONTENTS

CHAPTER ONE
GROWING UP
— 1 —

CHAPTER TWO
HIGH SCHOOL
— 15 —

CHAPTER THREE
THE MINOR LEAGUES
— 21 —

CHAPTER FOUR
THE MAJOR LEAGUES
— 25 —

CAREER HIGHLIGHTS
— 42 —

Mattingly's batting stance. He stands this way in the on-deck circle, too!

CHAPTER ONE
GROWING UP

What does New York Yankees super first baseman and hitter Don Mattingly do during baseball's off season? Does he travel to exotic places, eat at fancy restaurants, or buy a whole slew of cool sports cars? No, that's exactly what he *doesn't* do! Donald Arthur Mattingly spends every minute off-season at home in Darmstadt, Indiana, enjoying life with his wife, Kim, and their two sons, Taylor and Preston.

Everyone who's known Don from the time he was a boy growing up in Evansville,

Indiana (just south of Darmstadt), agrees that he has always been dedicated to his family. While money and fame change some sports stars, Don has managed to remain unspoiled.

He was born on April 20, 1961, in Evansville, the youngest of four boys and a girl. To this day, the entire Mattingly clan remains as close as ever. But Don will be the first to tell you that what brought him and his three brothers closest while growing up was their love and enthusiasm for sports.

"It seems as if all the kids did in our neighborhood was play sports from sunup to sundown," remembers Randy Mattingly, one of Don's older brothers.

"My dad coached [our brother] Jerry and me in Little League," Randy continued, "but even when he stopped, he always took time off from work to see our games. He never said much, but he and mom went to all our games; and since there were four brothers all spaced five years apart, that was some task!

"He also made it easy for us to play. When each one of us got to high school, he'd tell us not to bother getting a job, but to play all sports; and he'd find a way to keep us in a little pocket change. Growing up in our family, it was like you *had* to play baseball!"

Don remembers, too, how much he loved baseball as a kid. And lucky for him, he had three older brothers to teach him the game! "There's no substitute for learning to play from older brothers," he says.

Growing up in such an athletic environment, it was no surprise that he joined the local Little League team as soon as he was old enough. When he was ten

As a youngster, Don learned habits that he would take with him all the way to the majors.

years old, he played a memorable game at Northside Little League Park. During the first inning, Don came up at bat.

As he waited for the first pitch, he could hear his friends and family cheering him on, shouting, "C'mon, Donny! Hit it out here to left field!"

No one really expected Don to hit a homer because although he usually made contact with the ball, he wasn't considered much of a slugger. Imagine their surprise when he walloped the first pitch *exactly* where they had asked—over the left-field fence!

Don was so pleased with himself that he gave out an Indian war whoop as he rounded the bases! But his memorable game doesn't end there. In fact, he was just getting warmed up!

"Our friends got such a kick out of it," recalls Don's mother, Mary, "that the next time he came up to bat they yelled, 'Let's see you hit one over the center-field fence!' Sure enough, Don knocked the ball right over the center-field fence —and that was about 185 feet away! Boy, did he give a happy holler again when he ran around the bases!"

During his third and final time at bat, Don's family and friends couldn't resist calling to him once more. "OK, Donny," they cheered, "now hit one over the right-field fence!" And lo and behold, the youngest Mattingly did just that!

From that day on, Donny Mattingly was considered a regular Little League slugger. Never again did he hit three homers in one Little League game, but the word around town was that Evansville had a promising young baseball star, destined to become a big leaguer!

But Little League had its low points,

too. The game Don remembers most was not his three-home-run game, but a game where he did anything but shine on the baseball diamond.

"It was the first game of the season," Don remembers vividly. "I struck out three straight times against the same pitcher. I was so upset that I cried after the game. I was hurt and embarrassed."

"Striking out hurt him more than anything," recalls Don's father, William. "I told him not to worry about it. I told him, 'Go out and have a good time, and do the best you can. If things don't work out, forget about it.'"

Don promised himself that he would try harder the next time. "I told myself that it was just one game and that there's always tomorrow," he said. "I learned that failure is part of the game. You don't go out there to fail, but it will happen

With five Gold Glove awards, it's no wonder the Yankees have extended Don's contract for the next four years!

from time to time. It's important to learn from your mistakes in order to be the best player you can be." With such a healthy attitude, it's no wonder Don Mattingly eventually made it to the pros!

Little League baseball may have been Don's biggest passion, but following in the footsteps of his multitalented, athletic older brothers, he excelled in other sports, as well. In fact, he admits to playing nearly *every* popular sport at one time or another!

At age three, Don was chosen as mascot for his brother Jerry's basketball team! Even at such a young age, Don inherited his brother's enthusiasm for the sport. Often, toddler Donny would try to lift the heavy basketball, hoping to make a basket, just like his older brother!

Jerry also played football as a wide receiver on his high school football team, and baseball well enough to receive three professional contract offers. Unfortunately, he was killed in a construction accident at the age of 23.

Don's second oldest brother, Randy, was also an important role model for him. Randy played professional football in the NFL for the Chicago Bears, Buffalo Bills, and Cincinnati Bengals—and in Canada for four years.

And brother Michael, who is closest in age to Don, was a good enough basketball player to earn a scholarship to Indiana State University, where he played *both* basketball and baseball.

It's no wonder that Don has become such an incredible athlete—coming from such an athletic family!

Interestingly enough, there was a time when Don found himself playing basketball more often than baseball! "You had to round up too many guys for baseball," he remembers. "It was always easier to find a couple of guys for a game of two-on-two." Usually, when he got a game together, it was with his brothers and some neighborhood kids.

"There was such a difference in our ages," recalls Don, "that I was always one of the last guys picked! I was always used more as just an extra guy. But I played hard. I played pretty well and I always had fun doing it!"

But don't get him wrong—Don was, and still is, a fierce competitor. "It doesn't matter if it's Wiffle ball or chess," says Michael. "Don hates losing. I taught him to play chess when he was five. I wasn't bad for a ten-year-old, but he kept playing and playing and playing until he could beat me. He refuses to lose."

Because of his competitive nature, Don

wasn't happy being just a *good* basketball player—he wanted to be a *great* basketball player! He practiced long and hard at the game, and pretty soon he wasn't the last guy picked for teams, but the first!

"All the rest of us grew to six-two or six-four," says Michael, "and if Donny had gotten to our height, he'd probably have stuck with basketball."

"Basketball is really my game," says Don. "The problem was, the other kids got bigger and quicker—and I stayed short and slow!"

Playing basketball helped Don improve his *baseball* abilities. Since basketball skills help develop an athlete's coordination, Don used the sport as a method of cross-training—participating in one sport in order to enhance your abilities in another. To this day, he enjoys shooting hoops in his spare time, but it is written in his contract with the Yankees that he can't play basketball or racquetball—two of his favorite off-season sports—for fear of injury.

"I understand why they forbid them," Don says, "but I'm not sure it's right. I can do other activities for the physical conditioning I need, but I think it's good mentally to compete year round. I try to do that with my running. I try to compete in my lifting by pushing myself to the point of failure. But there's nothing like competition."

While basketball may have been the neighborhood game of choice in Evansville, the game the Mattingly boys always played was Wiffle ball. Don says that it was during those Wiffle ball "home" games that he developed his unique hitting style!

Don trains off-season by running every morning. It keeps him in tip-top shape for running the bases.

CHAPTER TWO
HIGH SCHOOL

By his junior year at Memorial High School, Don was playing baseball most of the time. "That's when it got serious," he says.

He continued to excel in other high school sports, but by then he knew "my running and jumping ability and size dictated that baseball was going to be my sport."

His daily dose of practice included coming home late for dinner every night in order to get in last ups before it turned dark.

In high school, Don developed the habits of patience and dedication that he would take with him all the way to the major leagues.

"He is the one kid in our family," says Michael, "who has our father's special quality—perseverance. Anything either one of them set their minds to do, they do."

"As a kid," explains Don, "you don't think of [playing baseball] as working. Even if you're improving your game, you always see it as playing. Just having fun." But it wasn't long before he realized that if he wanted to make it to the big leagues, he'd have to "work" harder than ever.

He credits his high school baseball coach, Quentin Merkell, for helping him improve his game. "He'd stay out until dark," Don says of his former coach,

Patience, dedication, and lots of practice helped Don make it to the pros.

"working with us, pushing us." For the first time in his life he began to understand the importance of practice. It was there, under Coach Merkell's guidance, that he began to see his hard work pay off.

"He [Merkell] taught us that we could always be better," says Don. "There was no getting a big head on that team. If you thought you were the best player in the school, he said to strive to be the best in town. When you thought you were the best in town, he'd tell you to be the best in the state. It was never enough. Never be satisfied; learn to keep striving."

That year, Coach Merkell built a makeshift batting cage in the gymnasium. "I couldn't believe it," says Don. "I could hit all day, all winter, and never have to chase the balls! I was up there [in the gym] during lunch hours, recess, free periods, and after school."

By the time he was a senior, he had reached hero status in his hometown. The year before, he had hit .500 on the team; and in his senior year, he topped that stat by hitting .552. With Don's powerful hitting, Memorial won 59 games in a row those two seasons! Unfortunately, they lost the state finals in Don's last high school game. But even though there was no last-game win, those two winning seasons landed Don in *Sports Illustrated* magazine's "Faces in the Crowd" section.

The issue caught the attention of New York Yankee's owner George Steinbrenner. When Steinbrenner read about the high school slugger from Evansville, he knew that he wanted 18-year-old Don Mattingly to join the Yankees ball club.

In 1981, Don was named Yankee Minor League Player of the Year.

CHAPTER THREE

THE MINOR LEAGUES

The Yankees were ready to draft Don right out of high school, but Don's father thought that college should be Don's next step.

"He felt that [my] getting a college education was the most important thing to do at that time," recalls Don, "so he wanted me to go to school. I understood the importance of college, but I had other plans."

The Yankees were so headstrong about signing him that they managed to persuade Don's father to change his mind about college. It was a tough decision for Bill Mattingly—but he realized that Don had a chance to make it to the big leagues some day.

Soon after his high school graduation, Don Mattingly was on his way to Oneonta, New York, to play in the minor leagues for the Yankees!

He began at the bottom of the totem pole, so to speak—the tough, trying climb through what is known as the "farm system."

Though Don was thrilled to be part of a professional team, what he remembers most about that first season in Oneonta was his first slump. "I thought I was going to hit .500 in Oneonta like I did at Memorial," Don said, "so I was down because I thought I was really struggling." He soon came to realize that minor-league baseball was much tougher than high school baseball.

After his first season in the minors, Don married Kim Sexton, whom he had met in 1976 when her father coached his American Legion team.

More dedicated than ever, Don continued to work hard at improving his baseball skills. He knew that the only way to move up to the majors was to prove himself in the minors.

According to Kim, that winter Don became a workout fanatic! "He hardly ever showered or shaved!" Kim remembers. "He just hit and worked out, hit and worked out. He was a maniac!"

Don climbed through the minor leagues for three years, until 1982, when he moved to the highest level in the minors to play for the Columbus Clippers. That year he even played in seven games for the New York Yankees.

Don was named to his first American League All-Star Team in his first full season in the majors.

CHAPTER FOUR

THE MAJOR LEAGUES

"**I** knew I had to excel to move on," Don said, "so I just wanted to move a little each year. When I finally moved up in 1982, it was a dream come true!

"The next year, 1983, was different. I knew I would get to play," he continued, "and I knew I had to do something. I had to show that I belonged on the major league level."

Stick Michael, a Yankees coach in 1984, tells the story of Mattingly's first full season in the big leagues, and how the New

York Yankees knew from the start that they had a star on their team.

"When we first talked about bringing him up," says Michael, "he wasn't a pull hitter, but we knew he would hit for average. Yogi [Berra—the Yankees manager at the time] and the coaches got together, and we discussed how many home runs we thought Don might hit for us. The general consensus was between eight and twelve.

"When we got him here, and he saw [Yankee Stadium], he looked around and made the proper adjustments. He went from being an inside-out hitter to being able to pull the ball. That year, he hit 23 home runs, and 35 the next year!" Apparently, they had underestimated Don's tremendous batting power.

In that first full season with the Yankees, Don captured a batting title, and the year after won the Most Valuable Player award. For some athletes, this would have made their career. For Don Mattingly, it was only a starting point.

"I don't set goals, or look at numbers," he says. "I stay focused by trying to remain consistent. Every year I just want to improve, to get better. When I reach my peak, then I want to stay there, to play at that level consistently."

Nowadays, he continues to wow 'em at Yankee Stadium—not to mention at every away game the Yankees play—even though back problems caused him to miss much of the 1990 season. It's tough to imagine Don Mattingly as the "extra player" or the "last guy to be picked," as he claims to have been as a kid. The Don Mattingly most people know has become a legend in his own time.

Don began the 1991 season with a bang to pull the Yankees out of an early-May slump.

In his eighth full season as a first baseman with the Yankees, he has a list of records, awards, and achievements that is as long as a Yankee Stadium home run! And that list continues to grow with each new season. Some sports enthusiasts have even gone so far as to say, that at age 30, Don is already a shoe-in as a future Hall-of-Famer. He has been billed as the latest in a long line of Yankee greats, joining former "Bronx Bombers" Babe Ruth, Lou Gehrig, Mickey Mantle, and Joe DiMaggio.

Don has remained the sincere, hometown, guy-next-door he's always been. He has managed not to let success go to his head. And although some claim that Don has developed a tougher attitude since joining the Yankees, he claims that that trait stems from all the tremendous demands on his time.

"I have hardened a lot," Don admits. "With everyone wanting a piece of me, it can be tough. I try to accommodate as many people as I can, but sometimes I have to say enough is enough. I had to learn to budget my time.

"It gets to be, with so many people, you don't know who to trust. I don't have that many close friends. In my position, sometimes it's hard to make friends. You feel like you can't let your guard down."

One thing is certain, however. The close friends Don *does* have (aside from his Yankee teammates) can be found back home in Indiana!

There are Chip Wire and Larry Bitter, who have been friends of Don's since high school. And Karl Ralph, whom Don calls "Fast Eddie" and whom he credits with teaching him the low-rider style of wearing baseball pants that has become a Mattingly trademark.

In Evansville, off-season, Don can usually be found at one of two places. If he isn't at home playing with his sons, chances are he's at Mattingly's 23—a restaurant he opened back in 1987 with his father-in-law, Dennis Sexton. Mattingly's 23 is a warm, friendly place where people come from all over the country (and all over Evansville!) to eat or just to hang out.

Don stops by three or four nights a week during the off-season to chat with the customers, sign autographs, or hang out with Chip, Larry, or Karl. There are sweat shirts and posters for sale at the souvenir stand—a portion of the profits go to charity—and if he's around, kids can have their pictures taken with Mattingly himself!

Don says that one guy who lives in Staten Island, New York, has flown in two years in a row to celebrate New Year's Eve at Mattingly's 23, and parents have come all the way from Chicago to make a child's birthday party something special!

"My idea for the restaurant," Don explains in a *Topps* magazine interview, "was to load the walls with cool stuff, different things, some maybe up there for no reason whatsoever. It's almost like a museum, where you come in and look through the rooms. You go in three, four, or five times, and there are still maybe ten things you haven't seen yet."

What Don is referring to is his collection of baseball memorabilia that literally covers the walls of Mattingly's 23. Bats, balls, gloves, photos, baseball cards, uniforms, and other collectibles from

An autographed picture of Mickey Mantle hangs on the wall at Mattingly's 23.

such baseball legends as Babe Ruth, Ty Cobb, and Pete Rose line the walls. There are also football, hockey, boxing, and basketball collectibles, since Don still has a passion for those sports, too. In all, there are more than 3,000 items—many of them autographed—inside Mattingly's 23.

Among the memorabilia, some of Don's most cherished items include autographed collectibles from his two childhood idols, Pete Rose and Rod Carew, and a Lou Gehrig bat.

In addition, there's an entire wall dedicated to some of Don's favorite people in the world—his family! This wall is filled with family pictures of himself; Kim; their two boys, Taylor and Preston; and his parents, brothers, and sister.

Don began collecting baseball cards as a kid, "but I wasn't very organized at it," he said. "I had a bunch of them, for throwing or flipping around. They were just for fun."

Today Don is much more organized with his card collection. He has dozens of them, old and new, all neatly placed under the glass bar top at the restaurant.

As for Preston and Taylor, well, Don says they're too young to be serious card collectors yet, but a dozen or so Don Mattingly rookie cards (worth nearly $30 each) have been put away for safekeeping until the boys are older.

One thing Don wants his sons to have is an appreciation for the game of baseball. But above all, he wants them to have fun playing any sport they choose.

At home in Don and Kim's red brick house, there's a play loft upstairs exclusively for the kids. Downstairs in the three-car garage, Don has his own "playpen"!

In the garage, Don has installed both a batting cage and a pitching machine for training during the winter. There's also a boxer's speed bag. "I watched Sugar Ray Leonard work on this thing," explains Don, "and figured it had to help me. It's great for my hand-eye coordination."

Some days, Don can be found hitting in the garage hours before sunrise. Other times, he waits until the boys are asleep to knock a few baseballs.

Ever since joining the majors, Don has been a driven, dedicated worker. Off-season, he works out by running, racing against a clock, competing with himself. In addition, he exercises at the Evansville gym. Since injuring his back in 1990, he has drastically reduced his strenuous workout schedule, and has significantly cut down his time spent at batting practice.

But off-season, Don explains, he tries to spend as much time with Taylor and Preston as possible. After his daily morning back exercises, he likes to fix the kids breakfast.

"I'm an early-morning person," he confesses. "And anyway, Kim has to be both mother and father for much of the season, so I don't mind at all."

Ray Shulte, Don's business manager, says, "Even during the season, when [his agent] Jim Krivacs or I want to do business, we have to go on the road with the Yankees so we don't infringe upon Don's time with Kim and the kids."

At one time, Don had enjoyed attending baseball card shows, autographing his card for fans. But he never

Don's dedication to the Yankees is one reason why he was named 1991 team captain.

got used to charging money for his autograph, and began to pass on attending the shows, saying he believed the practice unfair.

"He hasn't done a card show since 1984," says Shulte. "He was once offered a minimum of $100,000 to do a special one, but he doesn't do them anymore. He only goes to one or two dinner events a winter—and they're either for charity or as favors."

For Don, the money and the fame is not what baseball is all about.

"I've grown up and matured over the years, and [making] that much money can certainly change your life," Don explains. "It all comes full circle. This is my career, but I don't really see it as a job. I still have fun playing baseball. And when you're having fun, enjoying what you're doing, it's easier to work at it and get better. It all comes from just liking the game."

He does, however, get a personal satisfaction from donating some of his money to important charities. In 1988, he donated $1,000 for each home run he hit towards purchasing special mobile medical units that service underpriveliged kids in New York City. In fact, Don is a major contributor to a number of charities in both New York and Indiana.

So, you ask, what's this small-town family man from Indiana doing playing for a big-city team like the New York Yankees? While it seems that Don Mattingly would be more comfortable playing for a team a little closer to home, Don insists he isn't leaving the Big Apple.

"I don't want to leave New York," he explains. "Yeah, I'm a small-town Indiana person, but I love the excitement and pressure of playing in New York.

"When I was growing up, I was a Reds fan. I didn't know much about the Yankee uniform and what Babe Ruth, Lou Gehrig, Joe DiMaggio, and Mickey Mantle had done. Now I do, and I'd like to play my whole career there."

And from the way things have been going for him lately, there's no doubt that Don Mattingly will be wearing the New York Yankees pinstripes for a long, long time to come!

CAREER HIGHLIGHTS

- Hit .349 at Oneonta, 1979.

- While playing for Greensboro, led South Atlantic League with .358 batting average; named Most Valuable Player, 1980.

- Named Yankee Minor League Player of the Year, 1981.

- Named International League All-Star outfielder, 1982; made major-league debut with Yankees in September 1982.

- Hit first major-league home run, 1983.

- Led American League with .343 batting average, 207 hits, 44 doubles, 1984.

- Led majors with 145 RBI, 48 doubles; named American League Most Valuable Player; hit career-high 35 home runs, 1985.

- Led major leagues with 238 hits, 388 total bases, 86 extra-base hits, 53 doubles; had career-high .352 batting average, 1986.

- Hit six grand-slam home runs to set a major-league record; set American League record and tied major-league record by homering in eight straight games, 1987.

- Got 1,000th career hit on July 3, 1988.

- Won fifth consecutive Rawlings A.L. Gold Glove Award, 1989.

- Selected to sixth consecutive A.L. All-Star team, 1989.

- Named Yankee team captain, Spring 1991.